More Praise for Shelby Stephenson

Shelby Stephenson is the poet par excellence of the distinctive culture of Southeastern North Carolina. He sings the moods of mockingbird, ditch bank, tobacco field with an accuracy and fullness unavailable elsewhere, saving a way of life for us even as it is passing.
—A. R. Ammons

Stephenson leads us through the lay of his ancestral land. He gives voice to his place and its people and does so unashamedly, with passion and precision, and, yes, with real country music.
—Kathryn Stripling Byer

Shelby Stephenson has few equals and no betters on the poetry scene—as I see it—today. I am baffled by and envious of his comprehensions and compassion.
—Ronald H. Bayes

Shelby Stephenson can walk out his back door—even in his sleep, it seems, so tithed to the land is his subconscious—and see what lies hidden before our very eyes: in the roods and plowsoles, the tree bark and creek beds, in his beloved spectre ancestors forever singing in his head. He writes about the mystery of the dirt—what it yields, what it reclaims—with more precision and prescience than any poet I can think of . . . .Blessed be his wholly liturgical verse—the bard, the very voice, of North Carolina.
—Joseph Bathanti

poems

Shelby Stephenson

Press 53
Winston-Salem

Press 53, LLC
PO Box 30314
Winston-Salem, NC 27130

First Edition

Copyright © 2019 by Shelby Stephenson

All rights reserved, including the right of reproduction in whole or in part in any form except in the case of brief quotations embodied in critical articles or reviews. For permission, contact publisher at editor@Press53.com, or at the address above.

Cover Art, "Tribute to Dorothea Lange," Copyright © 2019 by Jacob Stephenson, used by permission of the artist

Cover design by Jacob Stephenson

Author back cover photo by Kate Whittington

Author bio page photo by Jeff Davis

Library of Congress Control Number
2019945790

Printed on acid-free paper
ISBN 978-1-950413-14-0

*to the memory of the slaves in the Nimrod Stephenson Memorial Cemetery—
may the Spirit of their singing rise—*

*to the memory of my sister Maytle Rose Stephenson Hollingsworth
in whose hand I first saw the citation for the Bill of Sale
of July, the Slave Girl*

to the memory of July, the Slave Girl

to Terry and David Vaughan

and always to Nin

Acknowledgments

These poems appeared, sometimes in different versions, in the following publications:

Anthology of Appalachian Writers: Wiley Cash Volume X: "Coffin," "Requiem for Strung Fish," "Tools"

Broadside (prepared by Linda Fox, photographer, NC Archives, Surry Parker Photography Collection): "The Trouble Not Just in the South"

Fly With Me: "Why Poetry: Why Ironweeds"

Grey Sparrow Journal: "The Clay Eaters"

International Poetry Review: "Obscured Freedom" (as "Recollections"); in chapbook *Finch's Mash*

Iodine Poetry Journal: "Epitaph for the Slaves Lying Across the Road in the Nimrod Stephenson Memorial Cemetery," "In the Packhouse, a Study Now"

Like Light: 25 Years of Poetry and Prose By Bright Hill Poets & Writers: "Extremism," "Today I Started Loving the World Again"

NCASA (North Carolina Association of School Administrators): "Writing History's Bargain"

Not My President: The Anthology of Dissent: "Walk with Me"

Old Things: A Poetry and Prose Anthology: "Coastal Plain"

St. Andrews Review: "The Old-Field Cemetery" (as "Family Graveyard"); in chapbook *Finch's Mash*

Shub's Cooking (Red Dashboard): "Croaker"

The Torch: "Longing," "The Old Barn: South"

Town Creek Poetry: "To Lee Terry" (as "Sonnet")

What Matters (Anthology); later in *Shub's Cooking*: "Stephenson's Bar-B-Q"

Special thanks to Todd Johnson, Executive Director, Johnston County Heritage Center, Smithfield, NC, for his help regarding history relating to the slaves.

Contents

Greatgreatgrandpap George Stephenson	1
Longing	5
The Old-Field Cemetery	6
Writing History's Bargain	7
Of Slavery and Humanity	9
The Old Barn: South	15
Coffin	16
Coastal Plain	17
Requiem for Strung Fish	18
Tools	19
Extremism	20
Pap George and Isaac McCaslin	21
Parting Curtain	22
The Slave Boy Clay	23
July, the Slave Girl	24
Nobody Knows	25
Hidden Treasure	26
Obscuring Freedom	27
Cow Mire on Paul's Hill	28
Nimrod Stephenson Memorial Cemetery	29
The Hired Hand	30
Why Poetry: Why Ironweeds	31
Gone	32
Today I Started Loving the World Again	34
March	35
Croaker	36
The Clay Eaters	38
The Henry Knight Family	39
To Lee Terry	40
Stephenson's Bar-B-Q	41
So Many Steps	42
The Trouble Not Just in the South	43
Walk with Me	44
Three Songs: Three Characters	46
Beneath the Grave	49
In the Wilderness	50
The Corncrib Shelter	53
In The Packhouse, a Study Now	58
Three Prayers	59
Duet	62
Epitaph for the Slaves Lying Across the Road in the Nimrod Stephenson Memorial Cemetery	64
Author Biography	67

GREATGREATGRANDPAP GEORGE STEPHENSON

I HEAR HIM now—my greatgreatgrandpap George. Everybody calls him "Pap." I will tell you how it all was, and still is, even as the first Stephenson came to America as *Stevenson* mid to late seventeenth century.

John Stevenson settled in Isle of Wight County, Virginia—he was the first one. John Stevenson and Elizabeth, his wife, had children, one they named John Stevenson II.

John Stevenson II married Katherine Wiggs. They had a son named Solomon who brought his family to western Johnston County, North Carolina, in 1766, probably for richer lands than the swamps he tilled in Isle of Wight County.

This Solomon Stevenson I and his first wife had a son they named Solomon II. The Stevensons farmed lots of land obtained from King George, 1767, through an original land grant.

Solomon Stevenson II was the father of David *Stephenson* who was born about 1774. On a piece of the original land, David Stephenson farmed all around Middle Creek, Beaver Dam, and what I call today—"Paul's Hill."

David Stephenson married Arey Johnson. They had eleven children, including my greatgreatgrandpap George.

David Stephenson died in 1851. He and Arey are probably buried in the Nimrod Stephenson Memorial Cemetery. No markers identify their graves.

Greatgreatgrandpap George Stephenson was born about 1813. Part of his story concerns Penelope Lassiter.

Penelope Lassiter married Jacob T. Woodall in 1826. They had four children. Jacob T. Woodall died in 1833.

Penelope's father started his daughter's husband off in the slave-business: *(19 Jan. 1833: Elijah Lassiter of Johnston County sells to Jacob T. Woodall, Johnston County, my son-in-law, for Natural Love & Affection thereunto me, moving a Negro girl, Silvy, ca. 11 yrs). Wit: James G. Woodall, John Barber—Elijah (X) Lassiter, February Court, 1833,* **Kinfolks of Johnston County, Volume II, 30, Abstracts of Deeds: 1826-1865, Elizabeth E. Ross & Zelda B. Wood.**

My greatgreatgrandpap George married Penelope Lassiter Woodall on February 14, 1835. Silvy probably lived on Pap's farm until Pap's death in 1886.

It is recorded that Pap had seven slaves in 1863. Silvy was about thirty-five. She was the daughter of slaves Geraret and Venus. Everybody called Geraret "Uncle Jart." Silvy was listed as worth $200.00. Slaves were evaluated based on the amount of work they could do.

Penelope and Pap raised the four children she had with Jacob T. Woodall. She and Pap George had ten more, including Manly, my greatgrandfather.

After Penelope died, Pap George married her niece, Mary, in 1853. She went by the name Polly.

The burying ground is named for Nimrod Stephenson, one of Pap's and Polly's children.

In the mid-1950s, Nimrod's son, Leonard, made over that oldfield graveyard. I remember him, bush-axe on his shoulder, even in summertime, strolling around the graveyard in high rubber boots. Now I know he wore those boots to guard against copperheads and saw-briars.

Unmarked slave graves in the cemetery's back part give the place a feel of original ground—unworked, unplowed, and mostly unkempt.

My greatgrandfather Manly was born in 1836, died 1912. He and wife Martha lie right close to Pap George out there in that family cemetery.

Manly served in the Civil War. A Confederate musket is carved in his tombstone.

My father, Paul *S R*, loved to tell the story how his grandpa Manly let him ride his shoulders. "Grandpa Manly enjoyed seeing me toting his musket and running around the yard, pretending I was turkey-hunting." Paul *S R* was ten when his grandpa Manly died.

Manly and Martha had six children. One, my grandfather, George William Stephenson, was born in 1871. I called him Grandpa. He was a "called" country preacher. That means he did not study to preach. He looked leathery, wore a mustache, and pretty much always dressed in black.

I was eight years old in 1946 when Grandpa William died. I thought he would live forever. I thought I would too. Grandpa was active in local churches, in what was called the "So-Sation." I never heard anyone pronounce that word "Association."

Grandpa William was a mainstay at Rehobeth Primitive Baptist Church I attended as a boy. He made his sermons dwell. They rolled around the pulpit in singsong swells.

Grandpa William was married to Nancy Barbour. They had six children, including my father Paul *S R* who had a twin who died shortly after birth. I can hear my father say, "Maybe he was me."

Shepherd, the oldest son of Nancy and Grandpa William, was a preacher too. When they both preached on the same Sunday morning, they went on so long my thighs are still stuck to the homemade varnished pews! I prayed they would stop and let Sunday dinner come.

Shep's sister, Mary, felt the same way, after she came along. Hubert was the next child, nicknamed Shorty. Then Walter. I knew Uncle Walter best. He was a natural-born fisherman. He could smell bream and bass bedding in Holt's Lake.

My father—William Paul Stephenson *S R*—was twenty-one when he married my mother, Maytle Samantha Johnson. She was sixteen, plump as a partridge, he would say. They had four children: Maytle Rose Stephenson Hollingsworth, Paul Stephenson Jr, William Marshall Stephenson, and me—Shelby Dean Stephenson.

My father said he got me by not pulling out soon enough.

When my mother was about to have me, she let it be known she wanted a girl. So she named me for Shelby Jean Davis, the Little Mountain Sweetheart. She was from Mount Vernon, Kentucky. With the Cumberland Ridge Runners, she went up to Chicago in the 30s and sang on WLS National Barn Dance and Hayloft Frolic. I came along in 1938. The little Philco must have danced on the table in the kitchen when my parents heard her sing.

The "Dean" is for Dizzy Dean, the great pitcher for the St. Louis Cardinals. My father loved baseball.

He enjoyed also any history about war, perhaps because his grandpa Manly served in the Civil War.

My father said he named me for General Isaac Shelby, Revolutionary War.

My wife is Linda Letchworth Wilson Stephenson. We married in 1966. We live across the road from the Nimrod Stephenson Memorial Cemetery in a brick-ranch house my father had built in 1952. I was born at home in the plankhouse now outback in the hedge.

In suspension's memory I see my birth-house being pulled back on big, round, hand-hewn rollers in early spring, 1952, two mules, muscular as gladiators, doing the pulling, "Uncle" Dave Johnson, Selma, NC, my father's checker-playing friend, managing the job.

The plankhouse stands right where they left it. Ashley Langdon restored it in 2003. That's the best thing Linda ("Nin") and I have done since we moved back to the homeplace in spring, 1996.

LONGING

SOMETIMES I SING along the edges to see how things stack up in taking stock, seeing the farmers in their fields, the slaves, the mules, plus the poor who are Have-nots in a past shaping now and

of a fabric here on Paul's Hill and across the road in the Nimrod Stephenson Memorial Cemetery. The dogs howl over destruction of sways and changes history forms: Long Valley Cricket and Long

Valley Jamie—Tony, too, Butler, and the rest of my father's thirty-five, including Slobber Mouth, and those named for movie-stars—Bing, Bob, Rock, Ginger, Bette: they keep their noses on track to

help me tell consideration's properties: income rises and falls out of dirt and Time's condensation to gauge and dust off information. Memory moves to incorporate what was a plantation's dark spot

Jart could spit on and watch his collards come up, there, at Old Jart's Jungle: the soil was black and that rich: may he labor for space from Pap George's plantation: let the children, all nineteen, feel vibrations

in water under docks somewhere in Africa many hundred years ago, as slaves assemble to come to Jamestown, Virginia, in ships jostling cries of women and children to make lives possible on the edge

lived right up to mid-nineteenth century, when the slave-girl, July, house-worker and servant, brought another world to me. In gulfs I keep starting the story. Away from what she finds for me to know and

imagine we shall not be moved.

THE OLD-FIELD CEMETERY

I KNOW I represent the bones
among the slaves' graves
spreading something in dying,
rocks for stones unmarked and rained on
all these years, Sheb's father saying:

Your greatgreatgrandpap George
Here his slaves
I should remember...

They say her dance was sorrowful
Because she had fan-feet.
Roasting potatoes in a brushheap
With her runaway husband,
She vowed to live with him in Finch's Mash forever.
Then came the patter-rollers ... he to his captain's farm ...
She to her place ... like mules.

We girls with strong, pretty legs
whose feet pointed straight
brought more money.

WRITING HISTORY'S BARGAIN

I WANT TO break out of this place and rush diversity with color, make a prism of fan-feet running toward a random lifeline Equality threads in a language for white-black-brown of things John Hawkins organized for the ship *Jesus of Lubeck* which became involved in the Atlantic slave trade to Isle of Wight

while birds return trees to dogs and dogwoods, too, the leaves towels bountiful as a kitchen rack rusting in Greatgreatgrandmother Penelope's kitchen, mystery tolerating zero straight out of services for the dead in the Nimrod Stephenson Memorial Cemetery, that oldfield graveyard where celebrations and

distinctions the wind picks up and corners decisions away from hang-knots ignorance, full of mistakes, swallows: *I didn't bring as much money on the block as girls whose feet pointed straight*. Sing on, July: straighten yourself up and shout! Your bones breathe for other girls and boys in the fields:

intention loads pages, without guns, whips, covers: interrogation's too serious to misshape economy: war-time's real as the lives of families scattering estates, begging for things to lighten up acknowledgment so that confusion might beauty find for Love and sunshine today down on

Greatgreatgrandpap George's farm. Buzzards circle and lap the woods. A red-shouldered hawk screeches wing-wide sun-ribbons for you, July, forever and always ten years old: may there be no retreat from gestures, motions, tinctures, years: though you might have lived to be only thirty-three, you make

images flourish among citations in Johnston County's Courthouse: co-habitation records number and bloom in hairlines receding into the Register of Deed's visor: vision conjures silver in the old Family Bibles I sold for Southwestern Publishing Company, Nashville, Tennessee: *Please tie your apron*

loosely: your wide straw's aslant your head; an overseer's coat flashes across your throat. Your shadow minces self-doubts: Mahalia Jackson sings "Steal Away." All our born-days form Justice's slack, some shouts in nightmares fools dribble, muttering in a choir: *She could be buried near a KKK*. A graveyard-dig could end up on the feet of words: athletic as Mercury, you are Goddess of Sandals Winged for Service; horseless, a messenger for sake of those who write versions of *I'll Take My Stand.* Windows widen directions for flowers to bloom in rock-crevices: assemblages embody Mobile Gas signs

of the Flying Red Horse that lowers its back for us to ride on out of Comfort to find the graves of slaves, anyone could swear, walking there, hear the sounds the footsteps leave—*free, free, free.*

OF SLAVERY AND HUMANITY

> *I hain't got long to stay here.*
> —from "Steal Away"

MY FATHER PAUL *S R* says one more time, "It's right hard to think about it. I tried to do the best I could. And that was not good enough." Even now, from his grave, he writes his epitaph, living on through me long enough to see the color line untangle from the slave-graves in dirt that seeps down where he lies in Rehobeth Primitive Baptist Churchyard in Elevation Township, wisteria circling Greatgreatgrandpap George's plantation-house. I want to let the old music tune, all the way back to the slave-ships stuck in water up around Jamestown, Virginia.

Those Farming Poets, Want-to-Bees, who wrote *I'll Take My Stand*? Their views link like trace-chains around lights with lanterns aglow shining SALE—July—the Slave Girl, Pap George sold for $413.25. I hear the auctioneer in my head now, even if there was not one: a noisy whine snarls bad laws. Consider that a girl, ten, might sense much at all, as a three-fifths-person, to signal the world at large. Slavery's trunk sprouts branches in oldfield graveyards.

Rufus Haithcock's life I could not clear in ten-thousand pages, given the run of Pap's vision. Slavery's sages may never explain Haithcock's life as service: unconvinced that Freedom could not enable him, he sold himself to Babel. The citation conjures Slavery—1864: The words baffle: *That, I, Rufus Haithcock, a free person of color of said county—give—my undivided Services* to Charles H. Snead—right on down into the end of legalese—*affix my seal*—tamped *upon the oath*. For Haithcock's family, his descendants, present and future, I pray, for he agreed to act *as if I were his slave: know all men* that Register of Deeds, T. Snead, set a price—*One thousand dollars*—(blurring the vision)—which is Love—for *the space of ninety-nine years*. Look what law courts! All the way to 1963—creating cases to race for pleas and sessions to share Truth's appendices. See *Deed Book A-3*, at the Johnston County Courthouse in Smithfield, North Carolina, without my rages.

Desiring to include mistakes containing omissions, actions, and longings within what's deemed "American success"—consider most any sound-bites on television shows. I think of a house-painter I knew as a boy. He would drink paint-thinner, if he could not get rotgut whiskey.

Pap George's father did some bootlegging. That love of homemade whiskey comes down to me. I always loved to taste the good apple or peach brandy my father kept for toddy before supper. In *Deed Book 2, Ross-Wood, Johnston County, North Carolina*, volume II, there is this entry: David willed son George, my greatgreatgrandpap George, some horses and "one still worm and cap," along with "affection," too, and some "natural love."

David Stephenson was not a Slave Owner.

July came to Pap George through Penelope, Pap's first wife. She was Jacob T. Woodall's widow. Penelope's and Jacob's four children's names were William, Eldridge, Martha and Gideon. Penelope's nickname was Pen.

Here's the roll call for Pen and Pap George—their issue: Manicy, Arey, Calvin, Emily, Manly, Mary, George Henry, Nazareth, Penelope, and Obedience. When Pen died, George married Polly, Pen's niece. Pap and Polly had five children: Elizabeth, Ann, Rebecca, Ellen, and Nimrod.

Pap George's son, Manly, my greatgrandpa Manly, was a Private in The War, D Company, 50th Regiment. He served the Confederacy until General Lee surrendered his forces to the Union General Grant at Appomattox Courthouse, Virginia, in April, 1865.

Manly survived the war. He loved to farm and to serve as elder in Rehobeth Church. I can hear my father, Paul *S R*: "Grandpa Manly learned me a sense of history."

My father loved to hear his grandpa Manly tell about being in that War Between the States. After it ended the Stephensons were "land-poor." They had too many acres to farm. I've heard tell how Greatgrandpa Manly gave away a lot of his inheritance, trying to help his neighbors.

For the love of music—and grace—I think Grandfather William was "called" to preach. He thrilled his followers at Rehobeth Church.

Shelves fill with papers, regarding family, land, slaves—right here in Pleasant Grove Township. Makes me want to leave the fields alone and take my lines, bait, and poles, and go fishing. Every full moon in May I want to shout for spring and the fishing holes.

I want to take the dogs and hear them bark for Fourth of July—until History sits in a corner.

In my holiday's bones, I'd like to wake July up to lighten my loneliness, for my mind's on the graveyards, especially the one across the road. The stones do not move.

I ridge tobacco rows in my head; the tobacco buttons out.

I wonder where Percy Bolling's grave is: somewhere in a field for lack of wherewithal: his family had no money; segregated desperately, they prayed for extra-good weather. The word was *Work*.

My father was a sandlot baseball player. When TV came to Pleasant Grove he'd light his pipe with Bell's Three Nuns Tobacco—"None Nicer"—and watch Saturday evening baseball's Game of the Week, his eyes lit up in major league baseball scores.

I hear his five-string, a Leo Master my sister Rose gave him. He plays "Darling Nelly Gray."

Here's a list of the "Separate but Equal" Schools in Johnston County when I was coming along. First the African-American schools: New Bethel, Four Oaks, Princeton, Wilson's Mills, Cedar Grove, Booker Washington, Simms, Green, Bethel, Micro, Pineville, Stewart, Union, Rocky Branch, Atkinson's Academy, Hodges Chapel, Ransom's Academy. And these more show what separate equals: St. Amanda, Watson, and Stony Hill, Long Branch, Montgomery, Piney Grove, Pine Level. *Compiled by Margaret McLemore Lee, Smithfield, NC, Johnston County Heritage Center.*

Now the Caucasian list, 1920's, *Compiled for the Center by H. B. Marrow*: Allen, Archer Lodge, Bagley, Banner, Barbour, Baptist Center, Batten, Boyette, Emit, Beasley Grove, Blackman, Live Oak, Brown, Clayton, Corbett, Corinth, Creech, Four Oaks, Grove, Hatcher, Elevation, Hales, Stanley, Holders, Glendale, Holly Grove, Jernigan Grove, Corbett-Hatcher, Jerome (later became the town of Micro), Johnson, Hickory, Moore, Selma, Hightower, Long Pines, Pierce, Mill Creek, Glenwood, Massey, Meadow,

Oak Grove, Ogburn, Wildwood, Pine Level, Niagara, Mount Zion, Sandy Nook, Parker, New Beulah, Pineville, Piney Grove, Pittman, Plain View, Pleasant Hill, Poplar Springs, Shiloh, Polenta, Poplar Grove, Rock Hill, Royall, Powhatan, Princeton, Royal, Oliver, Rehobeth, Smithfield, Yelvington Grove, Sandy Grove, Sandy Ridge, Pleasant Grove, Sandy Springs, Spilona, Steward, Stilley, Temple Hill, Thanksgiving, Thornton, Smith, Wilson's Mills, Zebulon.

My school was Cleveland (all twelve years), opened, '26; closed, '99. I was a sophomore at Cleveland High when *Brown vs. Board of Education* roughly exhausted *Plessy vs. Ferguson* to the point that it is commonly considered to have been *de facto* overruled. Seems like yesterday—1954—little more than a winter's day since Lincoln struck off those bonds and scattered slaves, their bodies and souls no more property.

I list Cleveland for sake of my graduating class of 1956. I got a War Bond that year for being named The Most Outstanding Student. I cashed it because I wanted nice clothes for college. If I had kept it (the bond was for $18.00) I might have some money today: instead I bought a light-brown, pin-striped summer suit at Belk-Leggett-Horton in Carrboro. I enrolled at UNC-Chapel Hill. The rest is almost history. My father wanted me to stay here and help him farm. He told me, "This farm will be yours someday."

Leaving my Triple-0-18 Martin guitar at home, I went away, bought the suit and lost my pants (I was running from a panty-raid—I did not want to get caught and go to jail). I got tangled up in a barbed-wire fence down below Cobb Dorm. I got a scar in my groin to this day.

July Fourth! Salute July, the ten-year-old—unfurl the flag: Ju-ly (Stephens, Holt, Jones), her whole family going way back, sweating hard times.

There were some big plantations in Johnston County. The Watson Family sold in 1861 more human beings than I list now, lots of slavery's ghosts; some first names of those 143 slaves sold: America, Angelina, Cloe, Catherine, Fam, Fanny, Rose, Gabriel, Obedience, Handy, Isaac, Judy, Wash, Lettuce, Mary, Peg, Sam, Isaiah, Selina, Shade, Stamp, Violet, Woody, and Yankee. See *Abstracts of Deeds: Kinfolks*, Ross and Wood, Volume II, Courthouse, *Johnston County, 1826-1865*.

Another plantation, not far from Paul's Hill: leave this place's longleaf pines behind and go east on Highway 210 and take a right on that stretch of Galilee Road off the ag-complex, a plain trace-circling plantation the slaves of Ashley Sanders farmed. Todd Johnson, Executive Director, Johnston County Heritage Center, told me that Ashley Sanders owned about 2,700 acres out there on that road and that former slave Lightfoot Johnson bought in 1871 nineteen acres on Arters Branch. When Lightfoot died, his widow, Wealthy Sanders, deeded a quarter-acre to the church. The people named it Galilee Baptist Church. It was founded about 1875.

O say can you see, too, the Old Slave Market, in Fayetteville, North Carolina's sprawl, the tourists reading the several plaques, circling slowly in their cars or walking around the auction block. They see the word, "chattel." I say it again, myself, and think of cattle, for sale. And I see in my mind the fingers flutter, rattling slips of figures from galleys of ships. The old people called the ship that brought the first slaves to Isle of Wight— the *Good Ship Jesus*.

Sometimes someone asks me, if there's a South: I know one: it's right here in Pleasant Grove on Paul's Hill, the graveyard, the back part, the slaves buried there, no markers, just sun to rise and set; maybe July, her heart up *toward* the ground, her face to Pap George, turned; not far away he's got a stone.

I can hear Greatgrandpa Manly say his pap George was so bowbacked they could hardly get him in his coffin. And though Pap did not "own" that many slaves, he did sell July and her brother, Clay.

I wear Paul's Hill's history like a scroll, going up into Pap George's imagination: he named some slaves for planets so he could remember their names. He worked the land according to the stars.

They say Pap taught school at a one-room schoolhouse in Elevation Township. Harold Medlin told me. A historian of local matters, Medlin moves me to name all seven of Greatgreatgrandpap George's slaves: First, Geraret. Old people called him Jart. Then come, hand-running, Venus, Silvy, Daniel, Sarah, the latter two, children; little Haywood appears with Marzilla, younguns, too. They said July's name as "Ju-ly"; that's the slave-lore. She was named for her birth-month.

The total valuation of those seven: $2,650.00, the document stamped, dated, and evoking heaven, "First Thursday of April, 1863."

I picture a dashing Haywood, eleven years old, his wagon, loaded with fodder aflutter from Greatgreatgrandpap George's breath; Marzilla, six, attends his failing health.

Daniel, go free, you're twelve; ready your sack, skip to the field in morning dew: the bolls weigh more on the balances at weigh-up time when the sun's a waffle cake true as the red sails tingeing your cottonsack. Mister Shade and you will soon feed oxen, out of yoke: rest with them without sorrow; this stormy night will be gone tomorrow.

We know well the folly of ownership: the sands the harbors jiggle no reasonable reason why history's a burden. And words aren't worth a nettle, a friend told me, his color a small dip different from my own: "If it had not been for slavery," he said, "we would have never met."

I think of July, her head back, smiling, her sleeves frayed near a hot washpot. She's helping Penelope stir pig-skins and cracklins.

July lived to be about thirty-three. She's listed in the Co-habitation Records as "House-worker." She died about 1873. I picture her toting her cottonsack, for she's always ready, any field her lot. Ever loyal to Penelope, she's auctioned as Thing, why? For What?

Time changes everything. No need to push for hiding places in Finch's Mash or seek a Runaway's Path to thickly brush or sing "Steal Away" to announce the lash to pieces should be ripped: harder times we cannot forget, though they may not ever come again.

The worst parts of the past? Slaves, like cattle, tagged in droves, herded, and even rolled in barrels of nails to hurt them.

THE OLD BARN: SOUTH

I RETURN TO the homeplace,
the long path down Magnolia Lane,
and find only the ghosts
of July and her ancestors.

I hear the spirituals that dance
over a century after
Homer Plessy refused to sit
in a Jim Crow car.

Plessy vs. Ferguson
cries from briefs: *do something*
toward carrying out
Brown vs. Board: I measure

my life against the white sheets
holey with eyes in the road-deafening
muffles warming and lifting
away violence and climax toward

the slippages of lovers
in sheets while wives swing
from bedlam to rage against
promises the *Good Ship Jesus* docks,

churning carry-outs
to bigotry among the big
oak trees swaying *the past cannot die*,
memory simmering with dangling tongues

deep in the wide swatch
of *I'll Take My Stand*,
trying to cry, "Why me,"
in the caught-loll-thirst.

COFFIN

> *Account Sale: By amount paid: N. B. Honeycutt:*
> *Coffin: Oct. 19, 1886: $12.50*
> —*Accounts of Sale of George Stephenson, filed*
> *May 29, 1886, Nazareth Stephenson & M. J.*
> *Langdon, Executors, recorded in Record of*
> *Accounts* No. 4, Pages 211 to 214

I AM OUT for a walk
Where Greatgreatgrandpap George
Left his grave
For my casual feet.
His fiction of ownership
Swirls in smoke
From a trash barrel.

A ground's legacy,
Tended by mowers,
Is like a museum,
History's outlay
In manicure.

$12.50 was a lot
To make a coffin
In 1886. What he sold

July for comes around
To property nobody
Could own any more
Than riffs The Near Myths

Wail out of high ground
Where Pap's seven slaves
Lie in sunlight and dreaming

Encroachments of
The song I lyricize
To line off bills
And personal scores.

COASTAL PLAIN

ON THIS PLAIN there are hills.
Fields and woods go
On for miles into history,
The family cemetery, the crest,

Plus the corner directly across
From the cemetery where Paul's Hill
Was not dozed when Maytle's new house
Got built in 1952.

I close my eyes on a scene:
1851, July, the ten-year-old
Slave girl, chops the cotton
And sings another Freedom song.

The persimmon tree's gone from the field,
Five acres square, I shot
A dove out of with my .22 Winchester
That has no trigger-guard to this day.

There were plum bushes along the fence
Between the field and the line, behind the cemetery,
Where I would linger and plop the plums,
Yellowish red: they looked like bruised balls.

The field was gutted yesterday within an hour
Or two, swarms of workers, chanting, yodeling
For sweet potatoes to fill the crates
For the big trucks parked at the end

Of the rows to haul away to market.
The John Deere and diggers, yesterday, gone.
The worked field rejects fixes
It settles in clods.

REQUIEM FOR STRUNG FISH

GREATGRANDPA MANLY DID catch and string fish
On a sycamore twig on Middle Creek
When he was a boy before enlisting
As private in The War Between the States.
He wanted to leave the big plantation.
Slaves, 1863, Valuation.
He saw July working at her station,
Washing clothes for Pen and situating
Pap George's nap with his pipe and slippers.
Manly's sisters and brothers worked over
A hundred acres: Emancipation.
Freedom, invisible, confused worries.
Martha waited long hours for his return.
A changed man, he fished Middle Creek's refrain.

TOOLS

MY PEN WON out in my schoolwork,
Though I studied Farming first.

My father understood sores on mules.
I made images my tools
To appreciate my father's moves.

I do not mean lack of body.
I am talking dirt and toddy.
Like Reddy Kilowatt he was destined
To cultivate Paul's Hill in gestures.

A real strong man, he did not strain or curse.
Drool fell from his cigar, his change-purse
Floppy in his pocket, empty of all,
Except preaching—his father was William.

Manly, the Civil War vet, was William's daddy.
Pap George and Penelope begat Manly.

Nineteen kids could work a plantation's
Living past in tune with a weigh-horse's
Balances, plus inheritances rived
Out of lumber cut in Beaver Dam Woods
Where I walk to keep from misdoing
By neglect. I awaken to tunes,
Bird-songs, early morning cow-moos.

A post-hole digger I still use;
A slingblade Percy Bolling etched *PB* on;
Greatgreatgrandpap George's anvil
Fits conscience on my shoulders.

My father closes his eyes on a checkerboard.
My pen I hold between thumb and fingers.
"Get with it," I say; my thought malingers.

EXTREMISM

TWENTY MEN RIDE on horses down the street,
The horsemen, prancing and wearing white sheets

Down empty streets. Far away settling ships
Siege the sand at Jamestown, surreal, adrift

Until each person, considered three-fifths,
Floods the past, homeless, with hieroglyphs

Of deep, wide-pressing waves high into shills
Of human beings on way to Paul's Hill.

Twenty rears bounce up and down in jitters
Designed by rumps and animal withers.

July, just ten years old, our Slave Girl, walks
Up to them. Their shields do not make her gawk.

She's proud to address them as she wishes:
"What are you doing?" Somewhere in all this,

Oxen, sheep, pigs, and road-buggies raise dust-
Ruthless arias, field and stream, while guests

Check into the Gabriel Johnston Hotel.
Suddenly the horses bolt, turn toward Hell.

The sheets undress the men and float around
Market Street in nearby Smithfield town.

A dog barks and becomes spotted Boogie,
A sign, my brother Paul's charm; the spooky

Whites the women use to sew aprons, sheets
For beds no longer stained and smoothed with feats

Power and barter fix for color: eyes
Roll to bulge, then weeping what Tidewater

Turns, flows and surfaces pain to quiver
The slave ships in the mouth of James River.

PAP GEORGE AND ISAAC McCASLIN

DON'T YOU THINK Pap George and Ike McCaslin could have started a
  marital office?
McCaslin could have advised women how to keep their husbands who decide

To refuse their birthrights and go live like the Nazarene. Pap George could
  have taught spouses
How to raise children to farm lots of land, unfenced in, here, and in their
  afterlives.

Consider "Delta Autumn": Isaac McCaslin lay in the tent: the rising,
  falling flap
Murmured with rain: the bear in the big woods, gone; Ike huddled on his cot.

He had given up hunting, almost; his prejudice would not let him be like
  Sam Fathers,
His mentor, who lived, holding on, proud to come from the Chickasaw.

My greatgreatgrandpap George? I wish I knew what he really thought.
I surmise he wanted to farm his plantation. He sought

To do that, obviously, with all the family he, Pen, and Polly raised.
Isaac? Childlessness. He got caught up in nays.

I hear the wind course through Isaac's hunting horn today,
As he tells an African-American woman, holding her baby,

To go North where she will pass for white, she and the child,
Descendants of Isaac McCaslin; looking down at him, she replies,

"Old man, have you lived so long and forgotten so much that you
Don't remember anything you ever knew or felt or even heard about love?"

PARTING CURTAIN

JULY WANTS TO skip down Paul's Hill—sing to the sky—
"Swing down, *Sweet Freedom Chariot*, and let me fly!"

THE SLAVE BOY CLAY

> *"Clay, about 7 years"*: *Sold to James G. Woodall, for $241.00*
> —*Kinfolks of Johnston County: Abstracts of Deeds,*
> *1826-1865*, E. Ross and Z. Wood, Volume II, 116

GIVE ME A standing pass and let me mean
      What I know from a single document
      Witnessed, February Court, 1851.
William and Gideon, Penelope's
And Jacob T. Woodall's children, signed—
      Sold—by my ancestor, George Stephenson.
      What happened to young Clay, I cannot say,
Wanting to believe he more than yearned
To be free from slavery when he worked
      At the Woodall's Place, Emancipation
Still singing the blues that troubles today
      In and out of Freedom's predicament,
His master, Jacob, Pen's first husband, dead,
      And the auction block heaping on Clay's pain.

JULY, THE SLAVE GIRL

      Citation of Document for her sale: *11th day of January, 1850, signed, sealed, and delivered, February Term, 1851—Johnston County Deeds Book, W-2, pp. 114-115, Microfilm, State Archives, Raleigh, NC*

MAYBE PAP GEORGE was caught,
Webbed and stuck in the times
Like one of these grand fall
And dangling August spiders,

Afraid he could not do different,
So took Pen's inherited slaves
And kept what Splendor?
A plantation on Paul's Hill?

Land-poor and needing Help,
He sold July to in-law Seth,
A Woodall, kin to Penelope's
Deceased spouse, Jacob T.

My greatgreatgrandpap George
Sold July for $413.25;
The rest is forged
In history never spent.

How long is the one winter's day
That runs the history
Of three-fifths, a race
Toward an evening sun's

Song in thrall-raising anthems,
Alerting a captive, this girl,
Who wears Economy
For what? The government?

NOBODY KNOWS

AN OVERSEER IS a busy lord,
He must keep up with his lash;
A mistress leans into her porch,
And looks at floors, ties her sash;
I turn my eyes toward the corn,
Tobacco, cotton—to grace the strap.
      Said July from her unmarked grave
      In the Old Stephenson Cemetery.

Since I am a good house-servant
For George and Penelope Stephenson
What else can I do but steal
Away from the fix I am in,
Here on what you call Paul's Hill?
I don't know much, never had schooling.
      Said July from her unmarked grave
      In the Old Stephenson Cemetery.

The singer's trying to tell the world
About me, my family—three-fifths—persons!
The public's slow to catch on
The past, especially since we helpers
Stay fixed like animals and fake groans,
Then stoop and hide like Harriet Jacobs.
      Said July from her unmarked grave
      In the Old Stephenson Cemetery.

HIDDEN TREASURE

POETRY—SINGING, I do love, along
With wonder of underground families
Across the road in the graveyard, alone,
Each to each, buried according to will
Of those and Pap George who wanted to own;
Growing among creekrocks, dogwood-bowers,
Human beings, Time, and real human bones.
          I fill the feeders with seeds
          The perches flower.

Of those I want to recall and imagine,
I've come to appreciate July best.
My field works and shapes pictures
In ways to shine imagination's memory
Toward bigger histories forming in time.
          I fill the feeders with seeds
          The perches flower.

Spectral gowns dance in fog-shelves waving
Over graves no diggers with shovels sing;
I want to press on, stand up, keep going,
Desiring to see and know until the thing
Itself runs rampant to root my heart in reeds
I touch and, fingering, play a prayer.
          I fill the feeders with seeds
          The perches flower.

OBSCURING FREEDOM

WHEN THE ELDERLY sisters surrendered the plantation house,
The undergrowth filled with redbird nests lined with cotton
They plugged in their ears the last years
They sat on the veranda and watched the birds
Lean in crepe myrtle and the cars drive up
Main and cross the railroad tracks,
Things the mirror over the washbasin no
Longer gives back, the sweetness of hours, gums
Going up and down, the evenings
Long and flecked.

COW MIRE ON PAUL'S HILL

THIS MORNING'S CHILL traipses the sun's
Name bright as bronze on the plankhouse
I walk through, again, uplifted,
Transformed in Truth's bulging-out guts

Tumbling the world's laundry, wash-out
Of entrails, leaves, old-aged women,
Their wrinkles swallowed up in streams,
Ferns, hickory, haw, poplar, ash.

I am not surprised by the guests:
Bugs, goose-grass, fox-moths,
Marked by that stake Greatgrandpa Manly
Drove in the corner after he

Walked home from The War to see
His eighteen brothers and sisters—
And father, Pap George, who sold July
Whose body's not fixed property.

NIMROD STEPHENSON MEMORIAL CEMETERY

THE GRAVES ARE minding possums in
Mere grins under the sedgy doors.
When past feeds present, it is pain
No document, time, or folklore
Can change—the beds of slaves and stakes
Stamped *Deferred* no space can retake.

They lie across the road, aged rocks,
Unimpaired, snagging little feet
Of moles, a stray dog's bony back,
One neighbor's pig that's out to eat
The stars, rooting briars for strength
That holds them there for vision's length.

Cauliflowering clouds blow mist
Into mourning, settling the stone-
Scarred families etched to raise
Prominence of ancestral bones,
Yet cannot quash July the wind
Keeps up, surfing mounds she aligns.

THE HIRED HAND

COMES FOR WORK, snuff-dust identically
Browned as the union-suit exposing need,
Not all for money, but to sling the weeds
And bare the character of his living.

The stems falling under his song in dust
Reveal consequences of Slavery,
As he could not swing and cut off its bonds,
Make himself more than one who shuffles home

With accuracy his bumbling delight
Among summer blossoms and even gait
Scattering the birds out of the hedges
He cannot name and does not acknowledge.

Always he loves blues that cannot finish
The misery a mold could never shape,
Some dark beginning powering a whole
History raging for a choice kinship

With people sitting in back of the bus
Or in line at a fountain marked "Colored."

WHY POETRY: WHY IRONWEEDS

    for Margaret and Phil Baddour

AGAINST THE CALLOUSED hands of slaves and hoes
Ironweeds work April's dirt
And hum under pressure,

Everything a break
Thrusting no quiet resurrection
Teeming with the hired man's blade.

A grunt of Sweet Society Snuff
He spits in a plume of moans
Lost longingly to be teased.

They grow, these weeds, like Love
Never forming clarity, falling in a lump,
Their little yellow blossoms fighting back the leveling yard.

GONE

GREATGREATGRANDPAP GEORGE AND
Pen and Polly, their nineteen children—
How can I not be set on the local,
The dial trembling *Zero* to turn walls
My leads knock down and break across,

The music measuring old ways
When human beings were kept back—
Forced to live within a mode successful
For the worn-on system of plantations,
Yesterday, today—the morrow craving Love:

No more planters burly-surly, especially
Those who tried to treat the minions hospitably.
Consider the manse: my father inherited the ways.
He died in 1981. Descendants of slaves lived in his big house
He moved out of because he wanted a mailbox
By the side of the road.

I want a box full of letters sketching
How our story goes around the globe
From Seattle to Santa Barbara, Abilene,
Shreveport to St. Augustine,
Buxton, Elizabeth City, Philadelphia,
Unity, Syracuse, Buffalo, Portland.

The letters keep coming back to me:
You sold a steer once, the tidings capsized
The notion that your boat would float life on the farm.

Well, I'm back where I started from!
Does that count?

You bet your baby-bib and your locks!
Hair will grow like that: my mother's thrift
Clings to scabs and sores; my past
Knows how my house-key
Fits brocades and laces of drawers,
Your ribboned letters, the pale blue, narrow band
Of your heart's tug to ransack,

For good, Lady the Heifer's stall
I put up to help wean her when she was a baby calf.
And so I come to you, my did-you-wrong heart above my head;
I care for smiles and a toddler's drool.
Fools rush around my socks, knaves,
Disguised mosquitoes, looking at my
Fortunes as keeper of daily records,

My beat an intent to create no mire,
My aim to tune a choir, contemporary,
Yet old as "I Gave My Love a Cherry."
What a happening—the moon, full
Over the tree in the graveyard
Where Pap George lies. His wife, Penelope,
Her niece, his wife, too; her name, Mary (went by Polly).
Where are those two wives buried?
With composure, in farmed-over fields of compost.
You cannot have your cake and Eve's too!
I ripple under crowns, unmute the measured
Notes poverty's conversation destines.

TODAY I STARTED LOVING THE WORLD AGAIN

I SAW BEATITUDE dip its height to lower
Truth, after the frozen water, icicles, terrain
Grew to light a prophecy I could breathe
In the storm which Nature readies
To glances my eyes force to sunbeams
Memory forgets and regains until Fate
Rests Imposition to let the children back to classrooms
After the bell has rung and their shoes
Scatter the crusts which cake
Their father's house to reveal the notches
Against the wall, as boys grow to manhood
And girls swing their locks high out of measure.
Every youth wants to rule the roost,
Shoo the chickens off their poles,
Chase opossum scrambling through the briars.
Every mother's child knows passions wing force fleeing
From weapons, until the bulk of humankind wins
And guns have no dominion in the home.
Art and love even mysteries.
Climate creates what spheres, unknown,
Might change from chaos into forces wholesome and wise.
I knew Percy, my Sancho Panza Ironweed Slinger Downer.
I knew him through his talent transcendent
As his snuff-spittle served the yellow flowers,
His appetite for slave's work a representation
Of Man ascending to soundness
Until the circle he swathed turned him to labor
For food as he mumbled in triumph
At last, the whole backyard leveling the mellow
Growing his comfort and safety promoted him again
And again to hum and sling the weeds.

MARCH

THE MONTH OF the windy hill, after storms
Knock power out and leave me little hope
My cell might keep longing for norms
The full moon wreathes in orange handkerchiefs,

Jupiter staying near. I see the sky
Includes the infinitesimal *we*.
Norwich Cricket needs grooming for weather
Warming future days yearning to be free.

March: go out to the Scag and start it up,
Mow the meadow for betterment and for
The purple martins, too, I first saw on
The 22nd, scouts, male and female.

The sheer weight of fighting grass starts in spring,
Saves me from sameness, gives a liveliness
To itches, yodeling, and memory.
Black and Gray want to pull the plows in dreams.

I need to see Percy at the door now.
"Do you have some weeds in the yard to sling?"
Ah! The question comes along before lawns,
When the barnyard around Paul's Hill grew wild.

Well, get the slingblade in the barn, I say,
Cut the ironweeds again. He shuffles off
Like someone seeking nonchalance in chores.
He seems small and singularly all things.

The Scag stays ready; I must be careful.
The hillside is steep and slides in the ditch
Create burdens which shift to worriment
That I should not take chances when I mow.

I do not want to clip the last flower.
Leave it for the dream the earth surely knows,
For the love of a certain girl,
And for the truth, solid, of things to come.

Tubers worm turns toward Middle Creek's bridge.
The sunshine marks and shifts the water's ledge.

CROAKER

THE HIRED MAN wore three shirts when he'd scythe the weeds.
He'd get hot and just croak—I mean make a fuss.
I don't think he thought about the heat.
He wanted to sweat, especially on Mondays,
After a long weekend of whiskey-drinking.
Like a frog he'd croak.

I always took a croaker sack to Middle Creek.
Called it a tow sack too.
It would snag on bushes in the spring.
I was in a hurry to get to the water—the freshets and the branches.
At the Mouth of Buzzard Branch I'd set my poles
And wait for a chub-robin to bite.

Fishy, fishy in the brook,
Come and bite my little hook.
I will catch you like a man.
Mama will fry you in her pan.

When I became a man I went to the ocean to catch the croakers in the sand.
I could never get over my love for Middle Creek.
The surf was enough to take me away from home.
Home always lived in my bones—even on Roanoke Island.
I'd wonder where "Croatan" might have been carved on the tree.
I wondered more for thirty-two years as I taught school,
Robeson County, North Carolina, at what's now UNC-Pembroke.
A highway-marker text near the school:

CROATAN NORMAL SCHOOL:
Est. in 1887 to educate teachers of Indian Youth.
Forerunner of Pembroke State University.
Building 2/10 mile east.

What mysteries abound up and down—whether the Croatan Indians might be Ancestors of the Indians of Robeson County.

History's never nice, especially when the people make it wrong, as is often
    the case.

Whose people these are I think I know.
By North Carolina Law let's call them "people of color."

Set prejudice adrift.
Classified, they'll have to fight to be human.
They'll be under an old system.
We will be within a new.
We will be in public places—
Restrooms, for example, six—for White Men, one;
Indian Men, one. And one for "Colored."
Separation, likewise, for women.

If six paths went separate ways in a wood,
Which one would you take to make a difference?
The law gets suited up and can't dress down soon enough for justice.
A lot of gasping happens in the throat, for people, who fight for freedom,
    develop hoarseness.

Several North American fishes croak dismally.
Makes me feel bad, standing in the sand, hearing that sound.
I think of frogs, the Robust Redhorse, and ravens.
Croaking surrounds us now the more.

THE CLAY EATERS

I

AND DUCK SAID: *When I'm sluggish and need pep*
I take my spoon and basin to Paul's Hill,
That road-bank filled with glory, the thrill
I been waiting for, the white, gray and pink,
With all those streaked yellow and green tints
Thrown into my eyes, better than any pill
My doctor could tell me to take and bill
Me, oh yes, Lord, makes me want to dance—step
It up and go, child; I have not slept
Better—sign from above—the good Lord's will
Is working wonders; that business, the spill-
Over thing, that eating clay's a sure bet
For constipation? Why, I can just take
It with my cup of tomato wine filled
To the brim—better—hush your mouth—my ills,
Gone—melts in my soul like chocolate.

II

She'd come to Paul's Hill with Minnie Burch, two
Prospectors out to spoon porcelain clay,
Then trudge back to my father's homeplace turned
Tenant house—lived with Percy Bolling who
Would not be seen digging for clay; he stayed
At his landlord's place, he would say, to burn
The wood the fireplace warmed; he'd spit and chew
Tobacco, keep the woodstove hot to say
The oven's set, when the duo returned
With the clay they'd bake into marbles new
As magpies collecting shiny objects.
The word *pica*? They neither cared nor learned.

THE HENRY KNIGHT FAMILY

EVERYBODY CALLED HIM Uncle Henry.
His wife was Mary and there was Lil Sis,
Plus a "grand" always called "Little Mary."
Lil Sis, especially, perfect goddess,
She was, looking back to see estranged troves
Adolescence senses instinctively.

The color line adjusts variety.
Hope comes wordlessly; the heart opening
Destiny, bringing outward clear into
Society's popular shades to thread
The past weaving vagaries outright—treads
Which stamp human life filled with mystery,
A force we get to verify the dregs
We swallow, while Bondage, that Cheat, seals deals.

TO LEE TERRY

LEE NEVER LIFTED the veil which I knew
He could; out of slavery, he'd come here,
At the backdoor-steps which held him from me,
Centuries since 1619, not afraid
To say to Mister Paul, "Sir, I need more
Work—I want to buy some meat at the store."

I was background, too, one boy who saw Lee,
Sticking out his chest, tightening his lips,
To lift a stick of tied, wet, green weed free
Of the Mayo tobacco-burners—tips:
With his right hand he'd poke—straight out—the sticks,
One after another, shuffling his feet
Around mountains in the barn's eerily
Creaking history curing every leaf.

STEPHENSON'S BAR-B-Q

O MEMORY OF the Pig Split, Gallows-tree, Gambrels!
The restaurants, the roasting pork—
The Word itself—*bar-be-cue*—
For every pig-picking picnic—
The Thing itself—not the
Loose-sizzling juice that shoots
Into an inmate's veins as he
Dies on Death Row—no—
I'm talking about Stephenson's Bar-B-Q,
Near Benson, the one with the red-and-white sign
Shining up that stretch of N.C. 50
A little bit north of McGee's Crossroads,
Where coupes, SUVs, tractor-trailers,
Sports-cars (my Miata), pickups
Park out front, the nandina waving *Come on in*!
No matter which door you go through
Sits *The* Block

Cut and scarred, disfigured with healing
Time; yet the block sheds no blood,
Though there was a period when
"White Only" was pasted on the door,
The past, the future—now—unrelenting with beauty.
Life puts on Art, scarcely whitening the shoulders
Stephenson's Bar-B-Q uses for its meat,
History's scarred and blackened treat
The color line holds to industry
What the soul checks for humanity.
I'm talking about the soul of pork,
The *soul* parked right there in that
Chopping Block.

SO MANY STEPS

I PRAY FOR changes beautiful, renown,
The mean vestiges of the Ku Klux Klan,
The piled-high rocks for the unmarked slave graves;
For my ancestors who farmed while July sang
To let the patter-rollers hear her raves.

THE TROUBLE NOT JUST IN THE SOUTH

        THE WORD "COLORED" had the scholarly
inefficiency of an all-white stand. It
was a box whose foam filled the distant
moans and cries of a man swinging on a limb:
        When the KKK rode in their pickup-trucks
it was the beat-nest thing, wearing them homemade sheets.
        I was at the basketball pole in the barnyard,
strutting through the dusk-lit goal to see the evening
star aglow over David's shoulder
and he said, "Shub, black people will be in charge someday."
        In the kitchen my mother was cutting
up a chicken to roll in flour and fry,
although I could not invite David Williams
to eat the pullet-feet I loved or the neck or
the back my mother craved, no, he could not come in.
        You wait and see, you wait and see,
all this past is medicine we swallow hard and wait.
        I stood my ground. *I'll Take*
My Stand I had not yet read. I crossed
the yard, tagged each oak tree root, an ancestor,
I said to myself, and let David alone to live
and die, his prophecy no soul could not deny.

WALK WITH ME

I

ACROSS THE FIELD at evening sun
I met him, heard his record
Of hatred; I wanted to run
The path back home, let discord
For separate races play on,
Out of my sight: men in outfits,
White with little holes for scaring ones
Whose right to live in peace is lit
Forever; consider these, born
Little babies in arms of mothers
And fathers; those babes, grown, spinning
Their shame to tease others
To views rampant
With a child's impressionable
Mind to chance
A play uncomfortable.

The man's days spent in working—
Hard, he takes to drinking
Cans of beer by the case; the thirst
Drives him to nonstop thinking
How to spread *White*, denying
Living's many colors;
Believing that, belying
Times, even in darkest hours,
He would practice hate.
He would plow his corn, hoe beans
In comfort and promise no day
Would come to see him drunk and lean
From beer into bigotry
To take his own life just
As if his John Deere could crush any sacredness
His mind might accept a wider world
Than his small farm could,
Including visions of those who came to America as slaves.
Folly kept
Him focused on the Klan.
Perhaps it gave him a sense of being.
Disesteem ran
His world with slurs he'd spout toward me.

II

A shackled history
Can turn bricked-up misery
Into negatives begetting evil,
So that the heart's
Safeway to civil
Rest may spark
Lies, scattered, not much sense
Remaining, if one wants to know,
For example, that July, the slave girl, washed and rinsed
Clothes, walked around the lowgrounds of this man's ancestors,
And down rows in the Gnat Field,
Picking up points the Indians left
Before the Trail of Tears would yield
Sacrifices humans left bereft.

I think often what July's ancestors
And her descendants must have felt,
Their dreams
Put off, just about lost their chance,
The overseer, little granting,
Since landlord and tenancy set recognition's
Proper treatment for races planted
Here to work for decades in sized-up
Restraints formed by somebody else.
I started to say I
Have seen the black and white of belts
Swung against flesh to deny
People from fulfilling something
Inside that wants out,
To live in flinging
Harmony, away from the run
To hell and back to make
A Ku Klux Klan record turn on
A spindle, what I shake to say,
I heard, once, after a walk at setting sun.

THREE SONGS: THREE CHARACTERS

I

THE RAVING STORM Trooper stuck,
But Grimm is my last name,
And I served my military
Before Hitler was the rave,
When good was not in any way
The evil I tried to save
The town of Jefferson from and carry
What I learned as special deputy.
From countryside to countryside stand up for order.

I never thought I was that bad,
You know, to kick doors in.
I wanted to show the white race
What it was like to stand tall; so I had
My gun the sheriff did not want me to tote.
The hell, I said, and so I shot
J.C. and they said I cut
That murderer's balls out.
From countryside to countryside stand up for order.

I might have, I don't mind to tell,
Somebody's got to strut for right.
And he'd killed that Burden woman, hell,
He might have raped her, too; if he didn't,
He damned sure thought about doing it,
Being since he was black
Or at least didn't know who he was a bit
More than a snake coiled to strike.
From countryside to countryside stand up for order.

II

My name is Joanna Burden,
I came to Jefferson, Mississippi,
To help the people of color.
I mean my little house was my domain
And my New England roots made me
The right outsider to see how
I could do some good to stop separation
Between the races all around.
From countryside to countryside stand up for order.

Though somebody burned down my house,
Joe Christmas, maybe I think it was,
I meant no harm, alone as a mouse,
Forlorn, wanting no past to nurse
My life no more, and so I chose to come
To Yoknapatawpha County
Where water runs slow through flatland,
As said the Count who once was Count No Count.
From countryside to countryside stand up for order.

Though I was a mess myself, I know,
I pity those who hate, even me,
One woman among the Outcast, that One
Who ran from himself, the foundling, the lost
Little boy whose foster parents twisted
Into versions of themselves, each of them,
McEacherns, bent out of shape, existing
Long enough they almost could stand their strictness.
From countryside to countryside stand up for order.

III

Come walk with me: I am Lena Grove:
Come praise my walking feet and my lover
Byron Bunch who worked Saturdays at the mill
To help people and to stay out of trouble.
I never fought or stood for anything that fell
My way: I just wanted to get down the road
A mile or two so I could start over to tell
What it was like to get there.
From countryside to countryside stand up for order.

Who was the person who killed Miss Burden?
Her name was Joanna, I think,
I don't know; Joe Christmas? Certain
People want to know such things.
I just want to be calm and happy,
"Serene," the man who made me said.
I like that name, and Lena, too, like the Bible
Says somewhere, a good woman, one of the first.
From countryside to countryside stand up for order.

I never thought of victory.
It was always August in my book.
I had my baby in that way, to be
With me and let me like each brook
I passed on my way to Tennessee.
I loved the music along the way.
I loved the countryside round Jefferson.
I loved the coasting trees uncut always.
From countryside to countryside stand up for order.

BENEATH THE GRAVE

I AM TIRED, said July, lying
Beneath this creekrock, my body
Beaten in name of slavery.
I've been in the big kitchen, safe,
Tending preserves I cannot eat,
As servant to Penelope.
She is nice to me: she cannot
Escape the plantation any
More than I can. She's in her grave
And I am in mine. Feelings get
Blurred. I was so young. Sold at ten
To walk these fields. The muse sees fit
To let me be the one who holds
Kinship with human life. My love's
For singers. I'd like to be a
Star God bowls mornings at daybreak:
Time splats hooey called ownership.

IN THE WILDERNESS

I

I GO BY what my teachers knew
Around the oak erasure-tree
Where Miss Apple circled her walk.
I was the duster fleeing chalk.

I follow these sages, women,
In early grades; they took me in,
Surrogate moms in many ways,
Ran homes and farms during the days
Until the long, yellow bus's
Long door swung open, without fuss,
Depositing me on Paul's Hill.
I find fun and inspiration.

II

I can tell you much more than list
The dark, almost mind-clouding mist
The mornings rode, schooling me, Sheb,
Banked out of Middle Creek like a chub
Or minnow spinning on a line
The live-long days to form a vine
That puberty slipped up on me
When I settled toward Poverty
Which followed me on beyond school,
My ears hearing no Golden Rule.
The "called" preachers of the pulpits
Sawed air—Elevation Township.

III

O I remember Brer Rabbit,
The briar-patch, his pleading habit.
I learned the tale from a Reader
In class, Miss Johnson, my teacher,

Her voice a wispy hope complete
As she carriaged the room replete
With girls and boys, a wilderness
Of sorts, outside our homes, naive
Fantasies carousing our minds,
That long second-grade making time
Before Death obtruded my dreams,
Carrying me to funerals.

IV

The third grade for me was real hard.
Margaret (Brown) Maron I heard
For the first time; now she will let
On I was Miss Higgins's pet.
I wish I owned Margaret's view
That year; maybe she felt a few
Visions and longings for the charm
Of her Willow Springs country farm.
I know I was a scaredy-cat.
Miss Higgins's triumph! My math!
The proof: I flatly flunked the course
In college—and law school too! My
Demise: Federal Income Tax—
No way in the world I could last.
I left the law—or it left me.
I let singing songs set me free.

Some names before the legal rife:
Fifth grade: Miss Jones, willowy, lithe,
Light, nimble; Miss Weston? My fourth
Grade teacher: on my card-report?
"Talking out of turn"—C—***Conduct***
She wrote in bold like that; I let
That bother me, since honor roll
I made until the fourth grade: toll?
I can't stop talking out of turn,
Plus glandular expansion burns
In my heart: I must go, run on

The eighth, though first I'll set the tone
Of sixth, Miss Weeks, and the seventh—
Miss Creech, the sturdy coach and best
For bringing out rational me.
The creative was not the thing.

The wilderness's roads all turned
To sports I did practice; to yearn
To see my fame light up marquees
At Cleveland School; oh, no squeeze
Play at ball could make me profound
As my quest; I am confounded
To play the TV for baseball
Games I enjoy; I sigh and stall
When the position of players
Like Josh Hamilton keeps layers
Of hype and money in big-time sports.
I turned high school toward other starts.
Departures scrambled me, alone,
All to myself to find what bones
I might pick and grow some meat on.
I'd like to keep Time when it's gone.

V

On the front terrace on Paul's Hill
I hold close the October's chill.
I glare across the road to free
Life beside Greatgrandpa Manly,
Near July's master-overseer,
My greatgreatgrandpap George—her dear
Self, July, the Slave Girl, rages.
She inspires these words for ages:

> *The ground's a harp strung with shadows.*
> *Killdeer shriek cries in soft autumn.*

October 14, 2013

THE CORNCRIB SHELTER

I

A FLURRY OF hammer-pounds
fans a century and three-quarters
and my greatgrandfather
(the father of my father's mother)
leaves his cobbler's bench for the

War Between the States, he called it:
Jim Burrell Barbour, so slow
he could not settle back
anymore for anybody to appear
at his side, for no one

could wait for him to light his pipe,
even as his house was burning down.
He moved, and moves, up into
chainey-bush trees, angles his musket
and sees into the long

hall history grazes again
and moves me to the next item,
a plow-sweep smoothed for days, weeks,
sunup to sundown, seven days
a week, the Sabbath

a breaker to deem and damn
evil beyond the hedges of Paul's Hill,
years before the actual crib
was built (say, around 1930)
and again now this morning.

Through gaps in my vision,
the bushes sway as in communion
at the Old Baptist Church
where Nostalgia does not rule,
where sin runs yellow
and woodsmoke sharpens the air

at the plankhouse in the mid-20s
when my mother and father moved here
for me to come into the world,
for me to see the items in this shelter,

name them, and bid you listen
in your rooms to rain and wind
the years bring to the wrack
of the one-horse wagon, the two-horse,
too, McCormick, loaded with corn

for the crib when I came along, 1938,
growing in the moonlight
the stream I flow when my hand
roves quickly to
sling away

the king snake snuggling
among the shucks, while a crowd
of women in scarves
strip hog-guts in February's
cold and sing their hymns,

prayers in conjuration of better
days, their hardly remembered
faces now a straggle
on a past I clear out
of the corncrib shelter:

a calf's
muzzle on a nail in one corner,
a wasp nest spent and loosed
from the congregation of wrenches,
backbands, one mule shoe, hames, bridles, reins

hardened out of the leather
which drew them alongside the mules
of my days growing up here,
Black and Gray, the heat in their skin
wrinkling with blood clots from chains

scabbing their sides and possessing them.
Josh asks (he's helping Ashley rebuild
the crib after the termites moved in
and gutted two sides): "What's the muzzle for?"
"To wean the calf with," I say,

"We had a cow, gave four gallons a day."
Ashley's hammer falls and the power-tool
blasts the air a puff of bladed spray,
a drugged rise on a trail
not yet smoking with bells ringing again and again.

II

I park my Miata under the corncrib shelter now.
I've put netting across the ceiling the loft comes to,
to deter the Eastern Phoebe and the swallow.

They've got to fight for a home, too,
just as the starlings surely will hasten
along to crown the arrival

of the purple martins from Central America
the end of February, while the wind
blows round the Miata like a mirror

looking for someone to walk by to check
the gourds I put up with Leo Thornton's help,
home for the martins for about five months,

the wrapped netting around the martin-poles
a pretty-sure challenge for the snake to sneak
through when the nestlings flesh and their smell

aggravates the serpent's sensors
and rat snakes, mainly, rampage to move their
neighbors, the martins, out, insisting

on eating the babies while the little fuzz is
a thing of beauty, feathers for flying
across this hill to their road of air

until, Christ!—they leave side by side
in a flock in August to return to the climate
in winter they love, the days softening slower

time laying down the road I travel,
we all go on, alone, I who shot all
birds except the mockingbird, cardinal,

bluebird, catbird, wren,
their presences now
without politics or hard times, sinking

me up in something natural as money
bringing on my vocation,
a vacation, day in, day out,

hymns to the first parents,
the birds, too, and the animals.
A lot can be said about history—

the slaves working the fields,
the black and white tenants
of the 1920s crossing the dirt roads,

bearing down on plow handles to get to the fields
of corn, even dance in middles, while the tassels
sing in wind over the piled high
mounds for the corn-shuckings, the cured
tobacco for the bundlings, all that past,
as now: CVS won't sell tobacco products

anymore, I think, as I see sticks of tobacco
hanging above the crib-shelter,
in the rafters, those sticks put there

because the stems were "swelled up":
my father thought in time
they would cure themselves, "kill out,"

so he could "hide" the impure leaves
among some grade better for loading
the truck to take tobacco to the Perk Perkins Warehouse

in Smithfield, to sell; like everything
else here on what he called "the plantation,"
the follow-through keeps principles unforgiving;

so he would stop a hole where the hogs
got out and say, "Son, let's go fishing."
I pick up a gambrel in the dust doodle-bugs work,

prop it in a corner of the shelter, the shaky poles,
the hanging hogs, *my* education as a child,
all that, and always, the men and whiskey,

the moving hedge filling with yarrow in fall
the chickens would cultivate after settling on nests
in baskets nailed to the corncrib wall,

earthworms under my feet, the dirt, home, rich.

IN THE PACKHOUSE, A STUDY NOW

IN THE PACKHOUSE, a study now,
With books and papers arranged how
They stand where cured tobacco leaves
Lie in corners among fall's peas;
I am done with tobacco bundling—I vow.

The bench which held us long ago,
The grades, the smooth sticks in the holes,
Jackie Robinson, Jolting Joe—
In the packhouse.

I hear a fiddler draw the bow,
And purple martins, Keats's odes.
The little birds fly off like fleas,
Our largest swallow, dark species;
I no more handle tobacco
In the packhouse.

THREE PRAYERS

I

REMEMBERING ALL THE wars I have known
And the mainstay I have been told about,
Out of Slavery, that past, never gone,
I catch up while the politicos shout
At one another like robotic heads
Chasing lines and flirting hands making beds.

My father said his grandpa Manly
Learned him a sense of history;
That is all, he said, I know now
And all I ever need to know.

Manly enlisted for Johnston County
In The War to fight to help save the South.
Happenstance could have placed him for the North.
Fate's a passel of History's arms.
At twenty-eight, he was stout, his hands strong.
He was part of something far from Pap's farm.

Signed up for War in 1862.
July was about twenty-one or -two.
To be free she waved goodbye to Manly.
The fight for her freedom? Without choice she
Might have hugged her mistress Penelope
And joined Manly on the road to Raleigh.

II

The slave's civil toward overseer.
The soldier salutes his superior.
Zeus turns into a sky-shine Ruler-Swan
And whams on feathering query a crown.
Finite runs silly; Infinity's stuffed.
Arms fold farewells while battle-scars run pus.

He looked down the road
And saw the devil coming,
Pulled off his overcoat
And beat the devil running.

We've said that Pap George had those nineteen kids,
Fifteen he fathered with Pen and Polly.
We know four more came from Penelope's
First marriage to Jacob T. Woodall.
He passed away in his early twenties.
Regarding babies then? Make a plenty.

What if we could just let skirmishes be
Free of big talk like conflict's shock-n-awe
And build and sharpen our democracy;
Plus let the guns collect musk and the balls
To shoot in them gather space, time, and dust
While we work to let the war-machines rust.

III

I wonder if our Manly Stephenson
Might have seen the war-time nurse Walt Whitman.
Manly's call to help came from lonesomeness
And from desire in Necessity's bin,
Experience beyond his place, Paul's Hill.
I wish I had records of how he lived.

He rode the train to Polenta.
Am I making this up?
Martha waited by the garden gate;
That's a lovesong I can relate.

I know Manly's son could not read or write.
Like his father, he was born to hunt—work.
Grandpa William felt called to preach outright.
"Grandmuh" Nancy, her eyes blue-crinkling bright,
Read the Bible to William every night,
For Grandpa could neither read nor write.

After The War was over, the Blue and Gray
Went home to work the farms and hunt the dogs.
What really happened I wish I could say.
The country changed: the graveyards got the bones.
Politics spewed, sides stewed nationwide.
Slaves sang and longed for Freedom's rolling tide.

DUET

SON. YOU WHO are not yet bent,
And you who are for fun well-spent,
Know what it's like to wake before sun
And salute the morning's run.

Father. Merton Byrd, all the boys, Shoog,
Lester, the dogs, too, Butler, Tony, Blue,
The pickup, the horn with its cracked tune,
The fox crossing the road, the hollering,
The women, Mary Vance, especially, brushing
Her broom to swish the dogs out of her Leghorn chickens,
The world separate as a ball not yet dropped
Into Pou Junior Coats's glove on the Cleveland School lot—

Sad to remember the graves among the trees
At Rehobeth, your mammy lying beside me.
I want what I say to be more
Than my grassy mound and some thoughts on scores
Of hunts. We've been there and done that—embroidery—
What lives spin to raise the groundswell
Here and count the progress overspill
Since your greatgreatgrandpap George farmed Paul's Hill
With nineteen children, Pen, Polly, and a passel of slaves.
I think of July, what she went through, all her born days,
Had to; I'm glad you are telling the world
About her and how her soft chin fell
The day Pap sold her for $413.25.
Humanity's not an adjustable wrench!
I sure wish I could have changed history.
I went on, after The War Between the States—tried to.

Son. You are grounded still among the things of the past.

Father. MAYTLE SAID: *Paul, why do you keep these dogs?*
And the younguns needing to be clothed and fed?
The red-tailed fox nor the gray is
Worth more than our family now with
What I see on this small farm.
Tobacco allotment's not much and my right arm
Hurts more and more from sowing soda between the corn
Rows. I strow it—full hum down the middles early morn.

O my Dumpling, I answered,
I come home to you and we romp and sing
Of children in the ring.
Your face flares up with King Arthur Flour.
Your apron smells like an old brush-arbor.

Ma and Pa, gone, the ones before them, too, I'll say,
And your family becomes fewer by the day.
I'll cut the timber in Cow Mire,
Sell it—and save enough to build a house on this hill.

Son. What did she say?

Father. What has come your refrain:
*You spend more money on these dogs, Paul,
Than you do on your family.*

Son. She smiles her old grin, familiar,
And says how she depends on you to go on,
On the hunts, I mean—and run the fox,
But let it dodge your dogs, especially Slobber Mouth.
She's on the fox's side.
Your Maytle's always been for the underdog, like Spike, the little feist.
She does not care if she does not get
To help you stretch on a board a hide that'll fetch
A dollar from F.C. Fur Company, *Chi-ca-go.*
That's the way I feel, too—oh
How I want to give every living thing a chance.
My heart still aches for Runaways who hid out in Roach Branch.

EPITAPH FOR THE SLAVES LYING ACROSS THE ROAD IN THE NIMROD STEPHENSON MEMORIAL CEMETERY

GOOD FRIEND, FOR sake of these, refrain
        From lifting the dirt over them;
Blest be the ones that let them breathe,
        And pray for those who stomp on these.

Shelby Stephenson was Poet Laureate of North Carolina, 2015-2018. His recent books include *Our World*; *Nin's Poem*; *Paul's Hill: Homage to Whitman*; *Elegies for Small Game*, winner of Roanoke-Chowan Award; and *Family Matters: Homage to July, the Slave Girl*, winner of the Bellday Prize. He lives at the homeplace on Paul's Hill, where he was born, near McGee's Crossroads, about ten miles northwest of Benson, North Carolina.

www.ingramcontent.com/pod-product-compliance
Lightning Source LLC
LaVergne TN
LVHW041345080426
835512LV00006B/626